AF605260

OUR HOUSE

Trudie Trewin Lavanya Naidu

A Scholastic Press book from Scholastic Australia

In my house.

On my bed.

With my head on my pillow,
curled up snug and warm,
I think about today.
Back go the covers and out comes a yawn.

My eyelids are heavy, my eyes scratchy and blurry.
I'm so tired!
It's early,
but I know what I need now.

A nice full tummy!
'Come and eat.'
I hear a voice calling.

When the sky changes colour,
I go outside to play in the treehouse
and swing on the swing,
while there's still time.

A hand signals.

That's it.

No more playtime.

And then . . .

Everywhere is busy.
In the bedrooms,
cupboards are opened and closed.

In the kitchen,

drawers are opened and closed.

Arms point to here. And there.

We build piles
with chairs, tables, beds and more.
People tramp in and out,
carrying heavy loads.

There are boxes
everywhere.

But soon,
just one lonely box
sits in the middle of an empty room.

I close my eyes and imagine us
laughing and playing there,
where now everything is empty and bare.

Our first house is so special.

CHIPS

Doggo runs from room to room,
confused, sniffing empty corners.
Big brown eyes stare at us. 'Where are all the things?'

We share a hug, with shiny eyes.
'I love you, house,' I cry.
We all hold hands
and walk through the door.

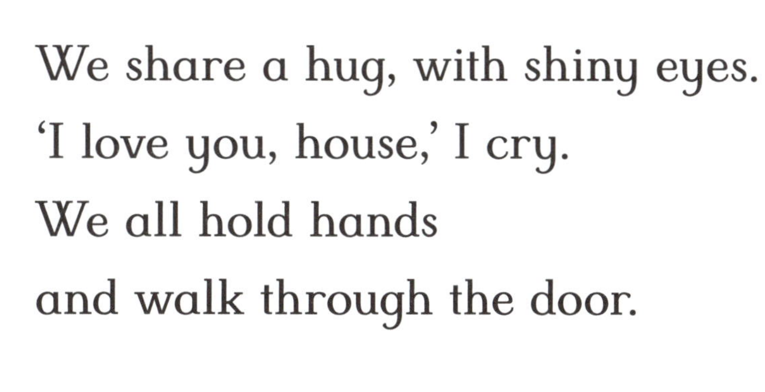

A new beginning . . .

We all hold hands
and walk through the door.
'I love you, house!' I cry.
With shiny eyes, we share a hug.

Big brown eyes stare at us. 'Where are all the things?'
Confused, sniffing empty corners,
Doggo runs from room to room.
Our first house is so special!

Where now everything is empty and bare,
I close my eyes and imagine us
laughing and playing there.

Just one lonely box
sits in the middle of an empty room.

But soon, there are boxes everywhere.
People tramp in and out, carrying heavy loads
with chairs, tables, beds and more.

KITCHEN STUFF

We build piles.

Arms point to here. And there.

In the kitchen, drawers are opened and closed.

In the bedrooms,
cupboards are opened and closed.
Everywhere is busy.

And then . . .

A hand signals. That's it. No more. Playtime!

While there's still time,

I go outside to play in the treehouse

and swing on the swing.

When the sky changes colour,
I hear a voice calling.
'Come and eat.'

A nice full tummy!

I know what I need now.
It's early, but
my eyelids are heavy,
my eyes scratchy and blurry.
I'm so tired!

Back go the covers and out comes a yawn.
I think about today,
with my head on the pillow, curled up snug and warm.

On my bed.
In my house.

For the BBs xxxx—T.T.

For Satyam—
no matter the place, with you, I'm home—L.N.

Scholastic Press
An imprint of Scholastic Australia Pty Limited (ABN 11 000 614 577)
PO Box 579 Gosford NSW 2250
www.scholastic.com.au

Part of the Scholastic Group
Sydney • Auckland • New York • Toronto • London • Mexico City
New Delhi • Hong Kong • Buenos Aires • Puerto Rico

Published by Scholastic Australia in 2024.

A catalogue record for this book is available from the National Library of Australia

ISBN: 978-1-76129-303-0

Typeset in Lunatoire and Organic Smoothie.

Lavanya Naidu created these illustrations digitally.
Designed by Nicole Stofberg.

Printed in China by RR Donnelley.

Scholastic Australia's policy, in association with RR Donnelley, is to use papers that are renewable and made efficiently from wood grown in responsibly managed forests, so as to minimise its environmental footprint.

10 9 8 7 6 5 4 3 2 24 25 26 27 28 / 2